My Heart; My Responsibility:
A Single Woman's Guide to Waiting

Daniellie Marie

MANIFOLD GRACE
Publishing House LLC

My Heart; My Responsibility: A Single Woman's Guide to Waiting
Copyright © 2019 Daniellie Marie

All rights reserved. No part of this book may be copied or reproduced in any form without written permission from the publisher.

Cover design: DeAngelo Gardner

Photographer: Daniel S. Harris

All Scripture taken from the King James Version of the Holy Bible

ISBN: 978-1-937400-30-9

Printed in the United States of America

Published by Manifold Grace Publishing House, LLC
Southfield, Michigan 48033
www.manifoldgracepublishinghouse.com

Dedication

This book is dedicated to my mom; Shirley Jean. You have shown me that love triumphs over brokenness, and purpose prevails despite pain.

Acknowledgments

I would like to acknowledge my family, friends and mentors for their love and support. With special thanks to my older sisters Ernesta (Nay) and Esther (Jennie) for helping me to become the woman I am today. I thank God for my spiritual leaders, my sorors and my team who labored with me. Thank you!

Table of Contents

	Dedication	v
	Acknowledgements	vii
	Introduction	xi
Chapter 1	I Am Not Regular	1
Chapter 2	A Diamond in the Toy Box	9
Chapter 3	Beauty in the Bag	19
Chapter 4	Found by Love	23
Chapter 5	Covered Vessel	27
Chapter 6	She Said Yes!	41
Chapter 7	Living Single	49
Chapter 8	Wait for It	57
	A Prayer for My Sisters	71
	About the Author	73

Introduction

Growing up, no one ever tells their young daughter she needs a boy to make her happy and complete. Yet it is often the message we see and hear as little girls, and a message we don't forget as women. I was fascinated by the idea of being in a relationship before I even understood what it really entailed. By the age of ten, I had created this fantasy world and everything about it was perfect. I had the full Barbie doll collection including the fully furnished house, the pink convertible car, her stylish clothes, and friends. And, of course, she had her man, Ken. Before I ever thought about a real boy, my fairytale began with my dolls.

In most Disney movies there is a princess being rescued by a prince. In super hero movies there is usually one special lady who captures the heart of the super hero. There seems to be a constant subliminal message that indicates a woman is better when she is with a man. Teen films portray the popular girl who is most likely to succeed as attractive, physically fit, and has a really cute boyfriend who is, of course, athletic. The girl who is portrayed as the smart, nice girl is usually oddly shaped, lacks fashion sense, could be socially accepted, but is almost always single.

As adults we often see the successful woman in film having multiple degrees, an executive position, a lavish lifestyle with great friends and a beautiful home; yet she is portrayed as unsatisfied until she has a man to share her success with. In religious affiliations, young women are taught to keep themselves pure and the Lord will bless them with a spouse when the time is right. However, what happens when that timeframe takes longer than you anticipated? What happens when prince charming turns out not to be so charming after all? Do you still believe in fairytales when you're still single and without the thing you desperately desire? More importantly, do you still trust in the Lord regardless of what it looks like and how long it takes?

For me, marriage had always been something I desired. In my mind it was the highest form of validation and acceptance from one person to another. There was something so attractive and special about this type of union. Somewhere in between being a girl and becoming a woman, I believed my life would be complete when I became a wife. I know this may seem kind of crazy, but hang in there with me. I hope to make it all make sense as the answers to these questions became clearer throughout this process.

Why was marriage so important to me? This is the question I began asking myself and discovered the answer was quite complex, and yet at the same time, simple.

I associated love, value and acceptance with marriage. Naturally, with this type of thinking I wanted to be picked for team marriage as quickly as possible. So, it's kind of like when you're waiting for the captain of the team to select you after tryouts or an audition. Typically, the most valuable players are called first to be part of the team. If not selected it has the potential to make a person feel as if they are not good enough. Some people may walk away and say "Who cares, I didn't really want to be on the team anyway". Others may maintain a positive attitude despite feeling left out. They may accept that the position just wasn't for them, or perhaps try again at another time. Then, there are those who have a really hard time dealing with not being picked and could perceive themselves as inadequate.

What happens, when you find yourself unselected and still waiting on your turn? For me, as long as I remained unpicked/unmarried (single), I believed the lie that told me I was not valuable or as good as the others who had been picked.

According to my plan, I would graduate from college, get married around age twenty-three and have my first child by twenty-five. I had it all figured out, right? But what happens when what you think you want is different than the Lord's will for your life? What do you do when His timeframe takes longer than you projected on your vision board? The only problem with my seemingly perfect plan is that it was mine and not His.

I said I trusted the Lord and declared, "Not my will, but Your will be done". However, the truth is I neglected to listen to that still small voice when He told me, *"Not now"*. To me, the Lord's plan did not make sense and was taking longer than I desired to wait. I became frustrated and fearful, which ultimately lead to doubt. I decided to take matters into my own hands. It never occurred to me, at that time, the Lord was trying to protect me, not hold something back from me. *The Lord will withhold no good thing from them who walk upright before Him* (Psalms 84:11).

For me, being single was like a bad disease that I desperately wanted to get rid of and the only cure was the wedding ring. So, I accepted the proposal of the first man who asked me to marry him. I knew him for only a short while and despite the warning signs and the leading of the Holy Spirit that told me not to do it, I wanted what I wanted. We met in May; got engaged in February and six months later we were married. Out of my desire to fulfill my plans, which were not approved by God, I entered into a marriage I wasn't prepared for. I rushed my process and if I am being completely honest, I didn't even know there was a process. I had not considered there were some things the Lord was trying to teach me about myself, and if left undone, I would be good for no one. There were some broken areas in my life that required healing. There were situations from my childhood I needed to address; otherwise my relationships would continue to be infected. What happened to me when I was a girl impacted my self-worth as a woman. I would continue to accept less than God's best for me until I understood what I was worth to Him.

No matter how many awards I received, or degrees I earned, I still felt a void and subconsciously I was trying to fill that void with the love of a man and the title of a wife. Our contentment and our identity must be rooted in Christ, because nothing else will be sufficient to fill our needs and we will remain incomplete. That is when I began to understand that my heart is my responsibility. I don't blame anyone for my decisions or the outcomes of those choices. I have learned that I must be responsible for the life the Lord has trusted me with.

As we take this journey together, as sisters and girlfriends, I pray you will find answers to questions you have had and seek God during this time of your singleness. If you allow Him, I believe He can make you whole, complete, and full. When you find peace in waiting and trust the plan of God you will be able to live a life free from anxiety and fear. May you experience and embrace complete joy and total contentment in the Lord.

Lord, I am nothing without you and I am honored that you chose a girl like me for an assignment such as this. I yield every part of me and ask you to take control. Lead me and guide me as I speak what you will have me to say in written form. May your word reach every person you intended for it to reach. Lord I ask that you teach us what is best for us and help us to wait on you. I pray my story will bring you glory and I thank you for allowing it all to work together for my good. In Jesus name I pray, Amen.

Chapter 1

I Am Not Regular

It was a cold afternoon. I was driving down Mack Ave. in Detroit, Michigan heading home from work. I was having a talk with the Lord as I usually do while alone in my car. I asked, "Lord, why do you want to use me? I am just a regular ole' person? There is nothing spectacular about me, nothing extraordinary about me; I don't have any super awesome talents. I am just regular."

This was the first time I realized I had not seen myself the way Christ sees me. I honestly thought my statement was an expression of modesty or humility at the fact that God wanted to use me. But the Lord's response revealed to me that it was a reflection of something deeper than that. It was a statement that uncovered how I viewed myself and shed light on the fact that I really did not think I was good enough to be used by the Lord.

The Lord spoke in an audible voice and said, *"Why do you keep saying you are regular? There is nothing regular about you, because there is nothing regular about me, and if I dwell on the inside of you – you are not regular."*

Then it really hit me because I viewed myself as regular, I allowed myself to be treated as such and accepted mediocre relationships. Where did this idea of me being "regular" come from and what did it even mean?

The word of God says if you seek, you shall find; if you knock, the doors will be opened unto you (Matthew 7:7). So, I began seeking the Lord about this. I wanted to understand why I viewed myself this way and began asking the Lord to help me change my perspective so that my thinking was aligned with His word. I came to discover I identified with feeling regular as a result of feeling I was not special. Despite my accomplishments, awards and amazing friends I still felt something was missing.

Growing Up Without a Mom or Dad

My father was incarcerated and I was living off 8 Mile and Livernois in Detroit, Michigan with my mom and her boyfriend, in his momma's basement. Little did I know, the world I knew would soon be shaken up.

It was the summer of 1994 when my mom told me I would be visiting my sisters in Taylor, Michigan. I was excited to see my sisters, my nieces and my nephew for the summer and thought they lived out of town because Taylor seemed so far from Detroit. I always loved school and began wondering when my mom would pick me up and take me back home. That fall I was enrolled into Eurekadale Elementary School in Taylor. I was confused and could not understand why I was going to school in Taylor with kids that didn't look, act or sound like me. I would rush to my sister's apartment from school and wait, with the phone, by the window with anticipation that my mom would return for me. Several years later my mom terminated her parental rights leaving my eldest sister as my legal guardian and me as a ward of the court.

This decision resulted in the ultimate feeling of rejection. Was I not pretty enough? Smart enough? If I was better would she come back for me? Did I do something wrong? These were questions I often asked but there were no answers; only empty spaces filled with more questions. Like, where is my mom? Why don't I have a dad? Did my mom and dad love me? If they did how could they just up and leave me? As a young girl, I thought if I wasn't good enough for them to keep me, who would want me? I felt my world had been shattered. Growing up, I don't remember us talking much about why my mom left or where my dad was. After a period of time, I became numb to all emotions and it was easier to feel nothing, rather than feel pain. I didn't realize the significance of their absence until I began asking the Lord to show me myself and the condition of my heart. The more time I spent with Him, He began to show me, this is where my view of regular stemmed from. Those unresolved issues from my childhood followed me into adulthood, without my permission and left me feeling incomplete and unwanted.

Make Me Feel Special

By middle school, I began seeking acceptance and inclusion within my peer groups. I joined various sports clubs to fulfill my need to be wanted and accepted. I was in the band, ran track, played volleyball and basketball. I was an honor roll student and my involvement in extracurricular activities kept me off the teacher's radar as a student in 'need'. I didn't act out, so I was not classified as a 'trouble maker'. I didn't hang out with kids that did drugs and skipped class so I wasn't labeled an 'at risk' student; but I needed help. I didn't want people feeling sorry for me; but I desperately wanted someone to take notice of the pain hidden behind my good grades, my school spirit, and my big cheerful smile. What people didn't see is, as a middle school student, I battled with suicidal thoughts and even had a plan. But God! His plan was greater than my plan and even though my silent cry for help went unnoticed by people, He has always been a present help in time of trouble (Psalm 46:1).

By high school, I found my identity in my uniforms, relationships, titles, and accomplishments. I was a varsity cheerleader, section leader of the band, member of the track team, and a student leader. I was a popular girl, with friends in all the different social groups. I worked two jobs, graduated with honors and was the first African American homecoming queen in Taylor, Michigan.

I found security in these titles and achievements and centered my worth within them. When I wore my uniform, I felt like I was somebody. I felt valuable, important and special; but at the end of the day when there was no more recognition, affirmation, attention or applause, I felt like regular ol' me again.

He said, "Don't do it", but I still said, "Yes"

Several weeks before graduating from college and moving back home, one of my college friends, my best friend, said, "D, don't marry the first guy you meet!" Looking back, I guess he saw something in me that I wasn't willing to see in myself. I did exactly what he told me not to do. Less than a year and a half later I was married.

I knew early on it wasn't a good fit. We were unequally yoked even though we went to church and served faithfully in the ministry. The Lord told me several times while we were dating to break up, but I was hard headed because I was fearful of being alone. I failed to yield to the voice of the Holy Spirit and instead followed my misleading heart.

It was the night before my bridesmaids and I were scheduled to meet with the bridal consultant to select their dresses. I didn't have the normal excitement I imagined I would have, instead I felt unsettled. As I got on my knees to pray, the Lord said, "He is not ready." I heard the Lord clearly, but I was too embarrassed to call it off at this point because the wedding was scheduled to take place in six months. I tried to reason with the Lord. I said, "Surely you can get him together in six months Lord, you can do anything."

He was attractive, personable, had good hair and was fun to be around. He made me laugh and said all the things I longed to hear, which made me feel special. Asking me to marry him was like a dream come true until I woke up!

Disobedience Leads to Destruction

We did look great in pictures and I finally had that ring, but it was not like the marriage I imaged with my Barbie and Ken dolls. Neither was it like the love novels I read or the happily ever after movies I watched. The idea of marriage seemed comforting, but the reality was, I still felt lonely.

There was a prophet who spoke these unforgettable words to me during the course of that marriage, "It's not your fault, but it was your choice." The Lord wanted me to honor Him through obedience, not through a marriage He had not approved.

Chapter 2

A Diamond in the Toy Box

Standing in the kitchen of my Grosse Pointe Park apartment washing dishes, I had a puzzling, yet profound vision. This is what I saw on that seemingly typical day:

I saw a child sitting in the middle of the floor surrounded by toys and there was an overflowing toy box, yet, surprisingly the child was not playing with any of them. Instead, the child was fiddling with a beautiful diamond. I could see the confused look on the child's face as he tried to understand what the shiny object was and what to do with it. The child eventually lost interest in the diamond and threw it into the toy box with the toys.

I began to analyze the vision. I attempted to make sense of what it could have possibly meant. The first thing I thought was, who would give a child a diamond and expect the child to care for it properly? My mind was racing to make sense of this seemingly random vision. I asked myself questions like; how did the child get access to the diamond? Whom did the diamond belong to? And, why wasn't the diamond properly cared for and stored in a safe place? I began to reflect on the time my sister, Jennie gifted me with a pair of diamond earrings. I was just an adolescent when I received such a valuable gift. Unfortunately, I did not understand the worth of those diamond earrings and, in my immaturity; I did not care for them properly. I lost them. I can imagine my sister was disappointed that I had not taken better care of what she offered me as a symbol of her love. I was not mature enough to handle such a valuable gift. I was negligent and irresponsible.

By this point, I had stopped washing dishes and was seated at the edge of my bed. I asked the Lord to show me what He was trying to convey to me. He began to show me that just like the diamond did not belong in the care of the child or in the toy box; my heart did not belong in the care of some of the people I had granted access to it. Like the child, when a person does not know or understand the value of something entrusted to them, they often misuse or mishandle it.

The Holy Spirit began to show me that it wasn't the

child's responsibility to care for something so valuable; instead it is the owner who is held liable to ensure its safety and proper care. The Lord was ultimately telling me that it is my heart and therefore the care of it is my responsibility. It was the revelation of this vision that led to the journey of self-exploration, healing and the birthing of this book.

The Lord began to minister to me concerning my heart and how it was like the diamond, which had often been given to childlike men. I began to see these men were not mature enough to handle, or care for me properly. As a result, I ended up in places I did not belong, such as a toy box. I had not realized it before that moment. I was hoping and expecting everyone else to handle my heart with care, but I had unknowingly failed to accept the responsibility of guarding my own heart. I had given my heart to those unfit or uninterested in caring for it and became devastated when my heart, like the diamond, was tossed into the toy box after being played with.

Speechless, I just sat there reflecting on the relationships I had been involved in. I asked the Lord to forgive me for being careless with the heart He had graciously given me. I also asked the Lord to help me forgive anyone who had, knowingly or unknowingly, taken a part of my heart and buried it in their toy box.

I understood the Lord was instructing me to be responsible with my heart, but in all honesty, I had no clue what that meant or how to do that. One of the blessings of having a personal relationship with the Lord is that you can talk to Him about anything and He will listen and respond. As I continued sitting at the edge of my bed the Lord began to give me a guideline consisting of three simple, yet insightful questions to help me determine who I should give my heart to. He simply said, *"Can you answer yes to the 3 D's: Does he Deserve it? Does he Desire it?* And *Does he know what to Do with it? It is your heart and your responsibility."*

<u>Girl, You Deserve the Best!</u>

You have likely heard it said, "There is someone for everyone." I suppose there may be some truth to this statement, but what I know for certain is that not everyone is for you. Some people simply do not deserve full access into your life, especially into your heart. *Does he deserve it?* This is a question I initially struggled with. It sounded like a prideful question and I thought, who was I to ask if someone deserved me? I wasn't quite sure what it was I actually deserved. The other challenging part was knowing if I answered honestly and the answer was "no" then I would be accepting less than God's best for me.

According to Merriam-Webster, the transitive verb of the word *deserve* means *to be worthy, fit, or suitable for some reward or requital.* I had to learn it was not only my responsibility to ask the question, but it was silly to avoid it.

I realized I was indeed the most appropriate person to ask this question because the quality of my life depends on it. To take it a step further, this question is not only applicable to a marital partner, but any type of relationship where I was being asked to give of myself in any capacity.

How many times have you found yourself in a relationship with a person you knew did not deserve your attention, affection, resources, or time?

Girl, there is nothing wrong with asking yourself if the person/people you are involved with socially, professionally, or romantically have the qualities deserving of you. Once you get to know a person, you can determine if you want to continue building the relationship or end it peacefully. It's all about choices and if you don't feel a person shares your interest, values, ethics and beliefs you have a right to keep it moving - and please do.

<u>Just say you want me!</u>

Desire seemed to be the least complex of the questions. After all, you'd know if someone wanted you or not, right? I initially learned of *The 5 Love Languages* (words of affirmation, quality time, receiving gifts, acts of service and physical touch) by Dr. Gary Chapman, when I was a sophomore at Central Michigan University. My primary love language is words of affirmation, so in order for me to feel desired, all you had to do was tell me how much you wanted me and how great you thought I was. I loved hearing how much value I brought into someone's life. The problem, however, was that people often said one thing, but their actions said something different. I was often deceived by vain words and empty promises. Yet, I held on to those words as if they were filled with truth. Hearing those words made me feel wanted and desired, because words of affirmation filled my love tank.

Some people need uninterrupted quality time to feel desired. Others may enjoy receiving thoughtful gifts as an expression of love. When genuine acts of service are done, some feel valued and others feel most connected when they are embraced, as their love language may be physical touch. Understanding your love language can enhance your perception of how you receive and give love, as well as, help you identify your areas of weakness or blind spots. Because my primary love language was words of affirmation, I had to be careful not to get caught up in what someone was saying, when they had no back up in their actions.

Desire should be demonstrated in both word and deed. I am so thankful God does not just say He loves us, but shows us in His actions too.

Our desires are liable to fluctuate and the things you thought you wanted at one time can become less desirable once obtained, or with prolonged delay. Have you ever wanted something so badly, but once you received it, you discover it really wasn't all you thought it would be? In fact, shortly after taking whatever 'it' may be into your possession, you came to the realization that it required more work than it's worth. Or, that it did not function properly, in which case your desire was to return the thing you wanted so badly. The Lord is aware of our current and future desires, which is why it is so important to trust His leading and not rely on our own understanding (Proverbs 3:5).

<u>What did I want?</u>

For so long I focused on making sure I was what everyone else wanted, I failed to ask, "Daniellie, what do you want?" Consumed with pleasing others, fitting their perfect mode, and being their ideal woman, I forgot about me.

The Lord is so good, because He began to show me that I not only have a responsibility regarding my heart; I have a choice. I believe the vision of the child sitting in the room full of toys, handling that beautiful diamond was a warning from the Lord. The warning; *don't to be so quick to just give your heart away to any ol' body.*

The heart can never be returned in the same condition in which it was given. Therefore, we must be responsible with who we give ourselves to. If you give yourself to people who have no desire for you and devalue your worth you may find yourself tossed in a toy box.

Handle Me with Care

When a package is shipped, fragile items are clearly labeled and protected to avoid the risk of being damaged. When we engage in relationships with people who are not qualified to handle us properly, we run the risk of being broken. My heart had been shattered as I had given it to individuals who did not know how to handle me with care. Just like it's our responsibility to inform the postal carrier our item prepared for shipment contains valuables that are fragile, it is equally our responsibility to first identify ourselves as valuable and also let it be known we need to be handled with care to minimize damage to our goods.

Before learning my worth and identity in Christ, I allowed people access to my heart without qualifying their ability to handle me with care. I can remember having conversations with my girls saying things like "Girl, you need someone who can handle you". But what did that actually mean, to be "handled"? I came to learn that being handled with force and aggression was not for me. Instead, I needed to be handled with care, gentleness, love, and consideration.

Because we are special and not regular, it is

important we take the responsibility of getting to know people before granting them access to our most prized possession; our heart. A toy box is no place for a beautiful diamond like you. With every position I have ever applied for there were qualifications that had to be met in order to be considered. If granted the position, there were then expectations to maintain the position. Failure to comply with the rules and regulations could result in immediate termination. While writing this book, one of the many revelations the Lord gave me was that we have a choice as to whom we allow access to our lives. Just because someone offers an invitation does not mean you have to accept it. It is our responsibility to properly assess the intent of those who express an interest in connecting with us and to determine if access should be granted or revoked.

Based on a person's actions and character, you have the right to decide if that person gets the reward of being in your life or not. Too many times we place our fate and destiny in the hands of others and hope for the best; allowing ourselves to go along for a ride despite not knowing the destination.

There is a difference between loving someone and granting them complete access to your heart. When you give your heart to someone, you must be sure they are going to take care of it to the best of their ability because it is delicate – it is fragile. I used to believe I had to accept anything a person offered me. At one point, fear gripped my heart and held me captive, causing me to stay despite being mishandled.

As I continue to grow closer to the Lord and discover my worth in Him, I understand why He tells us not to cast our pearls before swine (Matthew 7:6). I have the choice of waiting and keeping my pearls until the proper relationships manifest. Fear no longer has a place in my life. If you cannot handle me with care then you cannot have me.

Lord, I pray that you would give us a Godly boldness to disconnect from any relationship, partnership or business deal that is not of you. Lord, forgive us for looking to people and things to do what only you can do. Fulfillment does not come from people, money or things, only you Lord. Father I ask that you would give us peace regardless of our current situation. Lord help us to be responsible with where we take our spirits and our hearts.

Chapter 3

Beauty in the Bag

There was a beautifully wrapped gift box with a red bow on top and a crumpled up brown paper bag sitting on a table. The lid to the beautiful gift box was slightly removed revealing there was nothing inside. To my surprise, the crumpled up bag was filled with items of great value. The contents from the brown paper bag were poured into the beautiful gift box. This is what I saw one sunny afternoon while taking my dog, Mack Daddy, for a walk. I wasn't sure at that moment what it meant and to be honest the revelation of the vision continues to unfold.

The brown paper bag can represent a disposable item, while the gift box represents an object worthy of keeping. If I gave you a big gift box with a beautiful bow on top, I imagine you would carry it with both hands and handle it with care. You would likely be gentle with the gift not wanting to risk damaging it. I suspect if I gave you a crumpled up brown paper bag you would carry it with one hand before shoving it into your purse, handling it with less care and concern. The Lord began to show me that regardless of what I had gone through, including the mistakes I made, He still thought I was worth dying for and valuable enough to be kept.

Embracing and accepting the unconditional, unfailing, always abiding love of Christ is the most beautiful gift we could receive. When I was doing my own thing and living a life that was far from pleasing to God, He still saw the value He placed inside of me. He saw the beauty in my brown paper bag and He turned nothing into something, for His glory.

I believe God has invested unique gifts and talents within each of us to fulfill His purpose. We must know the enemy, seeing our value has made it his full-time job to steal our hope, kill our dreams and destroy the destiny the Lord has created for us. The enemy will try to cause us to abort our assignment by deceiving us into believing we are disposable and no longer valuable. The enemy told me that because my parents did not want me, no one ever would. I believed this lie for a long time and it distorted my perception of myself. This way of thinking resulted in being a pleaser of man.

I spent a long time trying to convince people, especially men, that I was good enough and worthy of being on their team. I desired to do everything possible to please a man because I wanted him to see how valuable I was. I tried to behave the right way, say the right things, look the right way, all so a man would approve of me. The truth is, the more I tried, the more rejected and used I felt. I did not see myself as a gift worthy of being handled with care; instead I allowed myself to be treated like a crumpled up brown paper bag. I am so thankful the Lord saw me when no one else could; He saw me when I didn't see myself. And He loved me enough to rescue me from every lie the enemy told me. Girlfriend, when you start seeing yourself the way Christ see's you, life has a whole new meaning.

<u>He Made Me a Gift</u>

The Lord had purpose for my life far before July 9, 1985. Before I was formed in my mother's womb, He knew me and had set me apart (Jeremiah 1:5). He knew everything about me, the good, the bad and the ugly, yet He still chose to love me. He took my brokenness, shame, insecurities, fears and doubts and began to transform me by His spirit and through His Word. I was no longer a hostage to my past, nor a victim of my pain.

The Lord set me free and I was determined to be everything He predestined me to be. The devil meant it for evil, but the Lord used it for my good and His glory (Genesis 50:20). He saw the beauty inside my brown paper bag and He made me a gift to be used for the Kingdom.

I believe the Lord allows us to go through challenging situations so He can purge, develop and prepare us for our purpose. He will remove the garbage from our lives and change us from the inside out. He will cause people to wonder how you went from being a brown paper bag to a beautifully wrapped gift with great substance.

In Christ, we truly can have it all and He will make all things new (2 Corinthians 5:17), including our outer packaging. I can truly say, today I do not look like what I have been through. Once I started seeing myself as a gift, I stopped allowing people to treat me like trash.

Chapter 4

Found by Love

It was a Wednesday night Bible Study, during praise and workshop when I had this vision: *a woman sitting alone, in the corner of what appeared to be a dungeon; it was dark, damp, and cold. Then in came a flashing light that reached out to her and lifted her up.* It became clear to me the woman I saw was me and despite the low place I was currently in, the Lord showed me the depth of His love and retractable reach. The most captivating part was that even when I wasn't looking for a savior, He rescued me. Regardless, of the condition or state you may be in, the love of God can find you and His strength will pull you out of any pit you're in.

Many times, in life our mistakes, disobedience and failures have a tendency to make us feel we are out of

God's reach and unworthy of His love, but this is not true. The love of God has no boundaries, no restrictions and His pursuit of us is relentless. I was looking for love and acceptance in people and His love was reaching for me the entire time; just waiting for me to accept the invitation.

I tried to find comfort in people and things to validate my worth I presented the best version of myself to the world; somehow, I thought the best version of me was connected to my status. So, there I was working overtime, trying to prove to everyone that I was a good fit for the position as a wife, a friend, a future mother, and a leader in the company.

I learned to conceal my flaws and put band-aids on the broken pieces of my heart to appear as if I had it all together. I didn't want anyone to see my flaws and insecurities, because I feared they would reject me if they really knew me. Before I knew it, the same façade I put on for the people in my life, became the very façade I tried to put on for God. Somewhere in my walk of faith, I felt as if I had to prove myself to God. Anytime you're trying to prove something to someone, you attempt to put your best foot forward but eventually the true you comes out. I soon came to realize the Lord, unlike people, was not interested in the best part of me only; He wanted all of me. Yes! He wants our insecurities, imperfections, failures, fears, and disappointments. He wants our shortcomings, our addictions, bad attitudes, and habits. He not only wants it; He is the only one equipped to completely carry it.

<u>Accepting Love</u>

God is not like man. Yes, we've heard this, but to really embrace and accept this type of love is difficult for the natural mind to conceive. How could it be possible for someone to know everything there is to know about me, and still love me? Seeing my flaws and still wants me; knows all my sins, and still wants to use me. The love of Christ has continued to look past our flaws to see our need for Him.

I thought surely this amazing love of God was extended to me because I was doing the right thing. But the craziest thing happened; I continued to experience this same unfailing love even when I did the wrong things. It was truly His love and kindness that drew me and caused me to repent whenever I did anything that was contrary to Him. I began to accept the love of God as a gift to me. Experiencing and accepting this type of love resulted in a security I had never felt and one I never wanted to be without. I knew for a fact He wouldn't leave me. I had already given Him plenty of reasons to abandon me, but He never did. It was His perfect love for a broken woman that rescued and healed my fragmented heart.

Kept by Love

I was nine years old and can still remember it like it was yesterday. I was sitting on the cold wooden bench in a court room, looking down at my dangling feet because my legs were too short to reach the ground. It was the day my mother terminated her parental rights and granted legal guardianship to my eldest sister, Nay. I can remember feeling rejected, discarded, abandoned and unwanted. While those feelings were very real at the time, the truth is, the Lord was with me even during that situation. According to Psalm 27:10, He made a promise that even when my mother and father forsook me, He would take care of me.

As I look back over my life and begin to think of all the ways the Lord has kept me, my heart is filled with gratitude. Whether I was good or bad, He never let me go. As human beings, we get rid of things we deem disposable; things that no longer have value. God isn't like that. He specializes in using damaged goods and turning them into masterpieces for His glory.

That's what He did with me! He took a girl who was lost and showed her a love that can't be explained. He took the broken pieces of my heart and wrapped His unfailing love around them until there was no more room for fear, worry, or doubt.

Chapter 5

Covered Vessel

I had a vision of a tall multi-colored glass vessel; the imperfections, flaws and damages were disguised by the adhesive dressings on the inside. At first glance, all you could see were the beautiful colors and unique style of the vessel. Yet, as I took a deeper, more introspective look I could see it was pieced together with super glue, duct tape and band-aids.

The Lord began to show me that the vessel represented my heart. My heart was fragile and wounded and instead of addressing the root issues, I kept covering them up. I covered them up with things that made me feel good, so I didn't have to deal with the fact that I was bleeding out. I perceived those who expressed their emotions and cried about their pain as weak, so there was no way I was doing that. When I was hurt, I would quickly bandage myself up and keep things moving, as if nothing had happened. Due to the fact that I never dealt with the things that hurt me, I eventually developed a calloused heart. I thought it was normal to feel nothing at all.

I was shocked by this revelation, because by this time, I really thought I was okay. I was working at my dream job, thriving in my business, driving brand new cars, looking and feeling better than ever. I thought I was living my best life. Thought I had it going on! All you had to do was ask me. I didn't realize I was walking around with patches on a broken heart. It was a hard pill to swallow initially because I really thought I was ok. Despite my success, I still was not living up to my fullest potential.

As I began to seek the Lord concerning this revelation, He began to show me that a broken vessel, if pieced together properly, could still function. However, it had limitations and would leak if not covered correctly. I began to surrender to the Lord and invited Him into my broken vessel and asked Him to make me complete. He began to show me, the only way the vessel would become whole was for me to remove the bandages and allow Him to fill the holes. The only way to fill the void was by allowing the word of God to transform me.

It was much easier to flash a big smile across my face and talk about the good things and pretend the other stuff didn't exist. It was much easier than doing what I knew the Lord required me to do, which was deal with the issues I had worked so hard to conceal. I was really good at fooling people, or at least I thought I was. I knew I couldn't hide from God so I decided to remove the bandages and let Him heal me from the inside out. I had to deal with it so I could be healed from it.

Removing the Bandages

I was accompanying a client at a follow up Orthopedic Surgeon appointment where she was scheduled to have her stitches removed. The physician's assistant removed all the bandages and dressings that surrounded her wound before removing the sutures. The client was in pain as the damaged area was treated, but this was a part of the process in order for her to reach maximum recovery. The orthopedic surgeon came in and gave us instructions to properly care for the open wound to prevent infection while healing and ordered medication for pain relief. I found myself sitting in that office with my client, realizing it was time for me to remove the bandages from the wounds of my heart and allow the master surgeon to operate on me.

There are many remedies we use when we're

hurting or in pain. From ointment to pain pills, we do what it takes to nurture our wounds. I learned through this process of life that some wounds and scars cannot be treated with natural remedies; no matter how organic they are. Some issues can only come out with prayer and fasting (Matthew 17:21, Mark 9:29). I was trying to use my intellect to deal with my issues and cultural norms to soothe my broken heart.

Shopping, eating, men, sex, drugs and alcohol are common things we use to provide relief in a time of suffering and pain, but those are temporary fixes. I found myself using short term solutions for deeply rooted issues. When the thrill was gone, I was still left with my issues and had perhaps added new ones. I required a specialist to uproot issues of abandonment, insecurities, low self-worth, fears and rejection. I tried to find my value in relationships and in my success, but when those things ended, I was left broken and my usual remedies could no longer hide my wounds. Through prayer, fasting, praise, worship, and the word of God, I was able to receive His instructions so I could heal and relieve the pain.

My Band-aids: Marriage, Sex and Success
Marriage

I never really understood why I had such a strong desire to be married. I thought about being married when I was playing with Barbie dolls. My Barbie and

Ken were married, and in my mind, Barbie was special because she had a husband. I did not realize it at the time, but I was still looking for acceptance, validation and love and I believed marriage would offer me the security of these things.

Growing up with the absence of both parents left scars on my heart that I tried to conceal with the band-aid of marriage. I was trying to fill the void of abandonment and rejection with a husband. I met him right out of college and we dated for less than a year before getting engaged and soon after became newlyweds. During the courting period, I was in bliss, not realizing it was all smoke and mirrors. It is important we trust in the Lord, because He knows what we don't know and He sees what we cannot see. Throughout the courtship, the Holy Spirit kept telling me *"No."* He kept advising me to break up, but I was afraid of losing the security I had so tightly wrapped up in marriage. I disobeyed and moved forward with my own plans. It was six months before the wedding and the night before my bridal party was scheduled to meet with the consultant to select their bridesmaid's dresses. The Holy Spirit woke me from my sleep with an overwhelming feeling of uneasiness.

That night marked my final warning from the Holy Spirit as He told me, *"No, he is not ready".* Instead of trusting God and obeying Him I tried to reason with God hoping He would change His answer. I said,

"You're God, and you can do anything but fail. Surely you can get him ready in six months". The Lord did not force my will, nor did He change His will to appease to my flesh. I ignored the voice of God and choose what I wanted, not knowing I was heading down a road of self-inflicted pain and destruction.

The security I was looking for in marriage was shattered with broken vows. The happiness I imagined was interrupted by the reality of hidden truths and secret lies. I thought I would fill the void by simply saying, "I do". I was wrong. The love I thought would be reserved for only me was freely shared with women who had no knowledge of me. The fun we used to have faded away into memories of the past. I was looking for marriage to validate my significance and the role of wife to affirm my value. I arrogantly dismissed the warnings and did what I wanted; not realizing our relationship had begun to dissolve before our marriage even took place.

Sex

Sex was a part of my life before I knew exactly what it was and way before I ever did it. My interest was piqued as a young girl by the things I watched, the music I heard, and the stories I read. I equated sex to desire and to be desired meant to be wanted. I think it is safe to say, everyone has a need to be wanted, but what we do to fulfill that need varies.

It wasn't long after leaving the marriage that I sought temporary satisfaction and comfort in men through sex. I was trying to use human contact to heal the infection of rejection. I found myself doing things I never thought I would, even things I despised others for doing. Some of the choices were permanent and the consequences were irreversible including a terminated pregnancy. As I continued to feed my lustful appetite, sin began to dominate my life. My joy began to die, my peace dwindled away and my self-respect was on a rapid decline. I felt further away from God than I ever had before.

As I gave my gift to a man who wasn't my husband, it was as if he shuffled through my beautiful gift box taking out what he wanted and returning the remainder back to me. Each time he left, he took a piece of me; leaving me with a remnant of the night before and the reality of what would never be. Instead of being satisfied, I found myself feeling more incomplete; questioning the value left inside. I tried to use sex as a band-aid to alleviate loneliness, thinking if I showed him how far I was willing to go for him, he would stay with me. Girlfriend, let me tell you - doing the wrong things, even with the right person, is no guarantee he will stay. But when you do the right thing, according to the word of God, you will not lose anything. Instead of filling the void of loneliness, I felt more insecure and disconnected from God. This was the loneliest place I had ever experienced. I learned in this season that trying to live without God was not living at all.

I knew what the bible said regarding sex outside of marriage. Instead of yielding to the Holy Spirit, I surrendered to my own desires and was drawn away by lust. That small voice that used to lead me seemed to eventually fade away as I continued to do me. Fear kept me living in sin even when I knew deliverance and freedom was available through Christ. I knew the Lord was not pleased with my lifestyle and a part of me wanted to change, but there was another part that enjoyed the short-lived pleasures of my sinful ways. I felt as if I was in too deep and could not just walk away. I was too ashamed to talk to anyone about my secret battles, because I was supposed to know better. The truth is, I did know better, but I had no idea how to win this losing battle. I was lost and living in a dark place where I became unrecognizable to myself.

But in stepped Jesus! My redeemer. My conqueror. My Lord and savior. My deliverer. My hero and my Father. It was as if He literally reached into the pit and pulled me out. You see, I was used to the Lord coming through for me when I was doing the right things, but I wasn't sure if He would still want me when I was doing the wrong things. The Lord showed me His sovereignty and reminded me that He died for me, already knowing everything about me (Romans 5:8). As I repented for the error of my ways the Lord literally became my flashlight, leading me back to Him (Psalm 119:105).

I learned in this season that there is no area of darkness that intimidates my God. There is no addiction He can't overcome, no habit He can't break and no wound too deep for Him to heal. The Lord extended his retractable reach to me and captured me with His mercy and love. There was something about experiencing the love of God at this level that changed my life and my gratitude forever.

It wasn't an all of a sudden moment, but over time I began to surrender sexual sin and all the issues that were connected with it. It was a constant fight and I continued to seek the Lord asking Him for help through prayer and fasting. I became stronger and stronger and was eventually able to walk victoriously in that area of my life. The desire to be wanted and accepted was filled by the love of Jesus Christ and the ultimate sacrifice He made with the selfless price He paid. Recognizing that God loves me so much that He gave His only son to die for me, changed the way I saw the value He placed on me. As I removed the band-aid of sex, I allowed the Lord to heal those wounds as only He can. My desire to please the Lord became the highest priority to me.

Success

Success is encouraged, celebrated, and often times

expected. Initially, it was difficult for me to see how my motivation for success had indeed become a band-aid for me. I wasn't trying to be rich and famous, although I wasn't opposed to it. It was the positive reinforcement and validation of a job well done that I yearned for to fill the holes in me. I became infatuated with the attention and the recognition. The acknowledgement of my success made me feel significant and valuable.

I was a girl who desired to excel academically and socially. I graduated with honors and after four years of being in both marching and concert band, track, and cheerleader, I won the approval of my peers and was selected as the first African American Homecoming Queen in my hometown. Subconsciously, I had become dependent on the opinions and approval of others. There was an internal pressure to be perfect so people would want me.

As a woman, I focused on being the best in my career and had secured a respectable position as a social worker even before graduating with my master's degree at the age of 23. I was mentored by the CEO of the company and often invited to be a part of large projects and executive meetings. I took pride in being the youngest and often times the only African American sitting at the table. My opinions were requested; my voice was heard and it made me feel like I mattered.

In addition to pursuing my career as a social worker,

I began my journey as an entrepreneur through direct sales. The opportunity offered me personal development and advancement; I quickly moved up the career path. Within two and a half years of my debut, I had moved into the top 2% at one of the top direct sales companies. I was making more money than I knew how to manage and I was celebrated at a level I had never experienced. I finally felt like an "it" girl – an "it" girl is one who seemingly has it all. At the age of 25, I was one of the youngest African American directors in the state of Michigan. I was leading close to 50 women around the world in my Dream Team. I had earned the use of two career cars, received bonuses, gifts, name brand purses, was invited to lavish parties and had access to an exclusive group of women; all because of my success.

My sights were set on going national with the company. In May of 2015, I left my full-time dream job teaching drug prevention to pursue my business. It was a few months later when the Lord instructed me to step down from my leadership position with the company. I thought surely that could not have been God. I loved what I did, and everyone loved me. Stepping down was not a part of my plan and though I could not deny that small voice, I could not understand why He would ask me to do such a thing. Why would He ask me to give up my business? I had worked so hard and it offered me so many fulfillments. I'd later learn the business wasn't the problem. The issue was my unintentional desire for the approval and affirmation I received from the success of my business. I used it to fulfill voids in my life that could never be filled with natural success.

I can remember saying, "Who am I without my director suite, the career car and my team?" I loved everything about my business and especially the woman I had become, but it was clear my identity had become embedded in my position in that company. I began to idolize my role, so much so, that when the Lord told me to step down, I was not willing to obey. Let me tell you, whatever the Lord is urging you to let go of, it's better to listen and follow His instructions, even if you do not like them, than to hold on and end up losing more later. I spent the following six months failing miserably at what I was once so exceptional at. Eventually, I was unable to maintain production and I was asked to step down. I lost it all. It was in that time that I came to know the Lord as my provider; I spent the next few months looking for employment and trying to make ends meet. It was through this humbling process that I realized I had been suffering from an identity crisis. I had been looking to people and things to determine my worth, when Jesus Christ had already paid the ultimate price for me.

None of us are invincible to pain and disappointment, it is a part of life. Yet, as we remove our bandages and allow the Lord to heal those desolate areas in our lives, we will no longer look for people and things to fulfill and completely satisfy us. Marriage, sex, and success were short term solutions to deeper issues of the heart. As I began to give myself to the things of God, He began to cover my shattered heart with His love, mercy and unadulterated word. As I removed the bandages from my heart, the Lord began to heal me of those wounds and scars I was once so acquainted with. I am no longer that broken girl. He took my shattered vessel and turned me into a willing vessel to be used by Him.

Chapter 6

She Said Yes!

I yearned to hear the words, "Will you marry me?" I eagerly awaited my turn to post photos on social media showing off my bling ring, declaring my answer with the famous hash tag slogan (#SheSaidYes). The longer I waited for that proposal, which seemed as if it was never going to come, the more frustrated I became. The easier it was for me to revert back to my old way of thinking. I felt like I needed something to do in order to help God. Silly, right? As if any plan I could possibly come up with would be comparable to His plan for me. I realized my focus was off, way off. And the Lord spoke to me in the most detailed vision I had ever seen to confirm that I would make another bad mistake if I did not be still and wait for Him. He showed me a two-part vision and it was clear the decision was up to me. The question was, who would I follow? Would I trust the Lord and say "Yes" to Him without knowing how long I would have to wait for the promises? Or, would I lean to my Intelligence, Emotions, Experiences or Cultural norms (IEEC) to make my decisions?

Part 1:

I saw a woman seated inside the bottom of a castle looking up with great anticipation and complete contentment. Initially, there was no one outside of the castle doors, then a man appeared. He stood at the top of the castle door with a gift box in his hand, preparing to knock. The woman was still seated at the bottom of the castle without concern.

Part 2:

I saw a woman inside the bottom of a castle. This time, however, she was standing up and pacing. There was an expression of panic and impatience on her face. As she began to look outside the castle, she saw her friends with husbands and children. She left the castle from the back door to go find her a man from a set of castles she could see on the other side. When she arrived, there were multiple spaces that appeared to be holding cells: the first one had a *boy, the second had a male child, and the third space was empty. She walked past the boy in the first cell and looked down to see that the third cell was empty so she took the male child. I could hear her say, "He will do". What the woman could not see was the man in the third cell was not there because he was actually on his way to her. When he arrived at the castle and stood at the door, she was not there.*

This vision took place in 2015, and as I continued my journey as a single woman, it was this revelation that reminded me of the importance of continuing to say yes to His will, His way, His selection, His purpose and His timing. In the first part of the vision the Lord showed me what happens when we, as single women, wait for Him. I can remember there being a certain calmness about the woman in the first vision. I wondered what she was waiting for; perhaps she had everything she needed and was resting.

In the second part of the vision, the Lord showed me what happens when we don't trust Him and when we rely on our own IEEC (Intelligence, Emotions, Experiences, Cultural norms). It's much like the situation with Sarah and Abraham in Genesis, Chapters 15-21. When the Lord makes a promise, we must remember, His word is good and He does not need our input, opinions, or suggestions on carrying out His plan for our lives. He only requires our willingness to follow

His word with obedience.

I wondered why in the second vision the woman selected the child and I was reminded of the revelation He gave me in Chapter 2. The child represents immaturity and premature decisions. When we do not wait on the Lord, we run the risk of doing things prematurely. If certain foods are consumed without being thoroughly prepared you could be at risk of food poisoning. If a meal is not seasoned properly there is often a level of dissatisfaction. The taste isn't quite right. The Lord essentially wanted me to understand that anything outside of Him and His timing would not be good for me and would ultimately make me sick.

I have never been one of those girls who was good at waiting, so this revelation with all of its truths would remain an ongoing process for me. Maybe that isn't struggle, but I knew this was a tailor-made word for me and I could not ignore it. Even though I understood the benefits of waiting, it was still full of challenges. I wanted what I wanted and when I wanted it. If things were moving slower than I desired, I had (sometimes still have) a tendency to lean to my IEEC and limited understanding. The Lord was taking me to a new place and He required me to take my hands off the wheel and just rest in Him. The Lord wants us to trust Him, even when we do not understand the plan. Giving Him our "yes" requires that we let go of the things we thought we knew, in exchange for His infinite wisdom and unfailing love for us.

I looked at my track record and I had to admit it didn't look so good. I figured I might as well try things His way. After all, He is God and He knows what is best for me. So, I said yes to His plan with the full understanding that it would require a little patience on my part. I have come to learn that when we say yes to Him, we will have everything our hearts desire and more. The Lord does not want to keep good things from those who walk upright before Him. So, if you don't have what you most desire just yet, perhaps it is not good for you right now. I would encourage you to reflect on a time when you took matters into your own hands instead of waiting for the Lord. How did that work out for you? Consider, and write it down, why it was difficult for you to wait on the Lord and how things changed when you said yes to Him and His will.

_____
_____
_____
_____
_____
_____
_____
_____
_____

_____
_____
_____
_____
_____

<u>Girl… Lose Control</u>

    I was tired of trying to do things my way. It was evident without the leading of the Holy Spirit, I could really mess some things up. I knew the Lord and the power of His might, but I had not allowed Him complete control in my life as I thought I had. There were some areas I still wanted to maintain control of. In particular, the area of selecting a mate. This is silly because outside of accepting Christ as our personal Lord and Savior, saying, "Yes" to a man in marriage is the second most important decision we, single women, will make in my opinion.

    I remember having my list of what my dream man should look like and the attributes he should possess. I can remember one day driving down the street and the Lord revealing to me that I had an appetite for poison and it was time for me to grow up. Many times, we have developed habits and desires that are contrary to the will and the word of God; which inevitability leads to our destruction and demise. *There is a way that seems right to a person, but the end is death* (Proverbs 14:12). I have discovered the only way to avoid destitution is to say yes to His will and follow the plans He has set for us in our lives. Besides, He has created us for His good pleasure and knows the purpose for our lives (Col. 1:16).

Saying "Yes" is a Process

I initially had a difficult time reprogramming my thought process. I had become used to doing things a certain way and getting what I wanted, when I wanted it. It is easy to say yes, but if your actions do not demonstrate the commitment you made, your words become meaningless. Imagine the man of your dreams finally gets down on one knee and pops the big question. He proposes to you and you say yes. You select a date for the wedding to take place. You stand at the altar and commit your lives to one another in holy matrimony. Then the person you married breaks their vows. How would you feel if someone says yes to you, but goes back to living as if they had never made that promise?

This is how we should think of our commitment to the Lord. Once we have accepted Jesus Christ as our personal Lord and Savior, we should be willing and ready to obey His will for the rest of our lives. When we say yes to the Lord, He is expecting us to follow His commandments, which ultimately leads to great blessings for those who walk upright before Him.

Surrendered – Sold out – and Single

I made a decision to surrender my will for His, giving Him my complete yes. I was determined to live sold-out for Christ, with no Plan B. This did not happen overnight, nor was it without many failed attempts and distractions along the way. We must understand that we will never be without flaws, but with the help of the Lord, He will perfect (complete and mature) us so we can carry out His will/plan for our lives (Psalm 138:8). I had to change my way of thinking so I could always give my Lord my best. I realized that being single was not a punishment and being married wasn't the ultimate goal or reward. For the first time in my life, I was content with exactly where I was. My identity was not determined by my marital status. My joy no longer came from being affirmed by another. I knew I was created for His great pleasure and I was ready to, not only say yes to His will, but also to the work He called me to do.

Chapter 7

Living Single

There is a distinct difference between a married woman and a single woman. I was making things more complicated by blurring the lines, trying to play the role of wife to a boyfriend. To be honest, I found it difficult to be just a girlfriend after being a wife for five years. The support, sacrifices, and the affection I gave was culturally acceptable, but not supported by the word of God. Look at how clearly the word of God lays out the roles of a single woman and a married woman.

1 Corinthians 7:34 *There is difference also between a wife and a virgin. The unmarried woman careth for the things of the Lord, that she may be holy both in body and in spirit: but she that is married careth for the things of the*

world, how she may please her husband.

There is nothing confusing about this. However, my intelligence, emotions, experiences, and cultural norms, my IEEC, resulted in me behaving as a wife to a boyfriend. I would become frustrated and even resentful when the security that was offered, only through marriage, was missing. Here I was giving everything I had to offer and getting the bare minimum in return. My relationship started to feel like a long-term internship with no benefits and no end in sight. This led to feelings of anger, resentment, and embarrassment. I found myself having to fight old lies and insecurities within myself that tried to creep up again.

People would say things like, "Girl, any man would be lucky to have you for a wife" or "You're going to make a great wife someday." They were words of affirmation and flattery, but they did not match my reality. You see, I was doing everything I knew to do to get the guy and while there was a lot of talk concerning marriage, that's all it ever was. If I was being honest with myself, I knew I was doing too much, but I didn't really know how to just be a friend without mixing in the duties of a wife. The Lord spoke to me through a vision on November 20, 2014 and I shared the vision as a live demonstration during my first Singles Conference in March 2015. The vision was profound and I didn't know it then, but I would spend the rest of my journey as a single woman understanding the blueprint the Lord had laid out for me.

It was around 5 o'clock in the morning and I was stretched out on the couch talking on the telephone. There were two separate trails adjacent to one another headed in the same direction. There was a woman on one trail and a man on the other. While walking along their individual paths they looked over and noticed one another. The man seemed to have been in need of something as he looked perplexed and had a sad countenance on his face. The woman, eager to offer her assistance, left her path and began to walk alongside the man. She grabbed his hand and looked to him for approval. She was hoping he would welcome her on his path despite coming over without an invitation. The woman neglected her own trail and continued with the man along his course.

It was apparent the man was distracted as he continued to look for something; paying little attention to the woman. The man and the woman continued on this path hand-in-hand stumbling and bumping into things because the trail was designed for an individual, not a couple. They arrived at the altar, stood in their respective places, exchanged vows, and said, I do. As the couple began to walk on their new journey as husband and wife there was much discord because they were two incomplete beings, now *trying to be one.*

Each person has their own path they must purpose in their hearts to stay on until they become one. Most times, in our human nature to express love, we try to walk hand-in-hand with the person we care deeply about. Thus, leaving our path and joining him/her on theirs, but God says, *"No, I need you to stay the course I have set for you during this time of living single. I have some more things I am trying to teach you, give you and equip you with before the two can become one."* The warning was clear... *"Don't think about cutting your journey short".* By doing this, we run the risk of being two incomplete beings, attempting to be one full person - and it will never work.

Praise Report: It's nearly four years later (11/10/18) that I write these words and I couldn't be more thankful. The Lord has loved me enough to keep me on my path as a single woman to complete me that I may be thoroughly prepared for what He has for me next. Thank you, Jesus!

Life is Not a Game

Have you ever played the kind of video game that requires you to pass the beginning stage before you're able to access the more challenging stages? In the game, you're able to collect new weapons to use against your opponent with each level you successfully conqueror. In a video game we have the option to restart as frequently as we need to, but often times, we're unable to move to the next level until we have successfully completed the current level. Life is not a game, yet there are many correlations we can pull from them. Following the rules is essential for winning the game. I wish it were my testimony that I followed the instructions of the Lord precisely and remained on my path the entire time, without deviating and without disobedience, but that's just not my truth. Like in a video game, I found myself walking into traps I knew were there and sometimes destroying myself with the weapons that were supposed to be used on the enemy. I found myself often having to be reminded that my journey as a single woman was one I could not rush, and one I would have to endure independently. I was re-routed through repentance more times than I am proud to admit, but I was determined to stay my course until completion. Taking all the tools I acquired into the next stage.

Single and Satisfied

I no longer wanted to rush the process and I embraced my journey as a single woman. I decided to maximize my season of singleness instead of dreading it. When we are able to view our current position in life as a gift and not a punishment, we can find contentment in any situation. I was able to commit myself totally unto the Lord with minimal distractions. I offered Him my attention, affection, gifts and talents to advance the kingdom of God. We have a responsibility to live a life pleasing unto the Lord. I spent countless years trying to please myself and others and I decided it was time for me to live my life for an audience of one and that one is Jesus Christ - My Lord and Savior.

In addition to spending intimate time with the Lord through prayer, reading His word and fasting, I found it was also important to spend time with myself, family, and friends. Shakespeare said, "To thy own self be true", but how can we be true to ourselves when we don't even know ourselves. As single women, we have the privilege of not only getting to know the Lord, but taking a deeper look into ourselves. Who am I? What is my purpose? What type of things do I enjoy doing? What are my triggers and hot buttons? These are just a few questions I encourage you to ask yourself, but don't stop there. If you enjoy traveling, get your passport and travel. If you enjoy reading spend time daily reading and journaling.

Reading helped me better understand myself and my interactions with others. Learning these tools as a single woman can help you become effective in fulfilling your assignment and connecting with others.

For a long time, marriage was my highest priority. If you looked at any vision board I completed, marriage and family was at the top of my goal list. Let me be clear however, there is nothing wrong with wanting to be married or having a family, but when I realized there was more for me to accomplish as a single woman, I was able to shift my focus. Completing my assignment and pleasing the Father became my ultimate desire. There were some things I talked about doing, but for one reason or another I had not done. So, as a single woman I decided to develop and pursue my single goals. My goals are categorized as follows:

Spiritual
Fitness/Health
Finance
Ownership
Travel
Career Goals
Relationships (Family/friends/sisterhood)

Working on my single goals helped me remain faithful, fruitful, focused and fulfilled.

Chapter 8

Wait for It

As long as I knew the timeframe and the deadline of what I was expecting and working for, I had minimal resistance to the waiting process. While I was in school, I knew there were only two years of middle school before transitioning into high school. In high school, I knew the date of graduation and I was able to focus and stay preoccupied until that day finally came. In college, I knew the courses that needed to be taken and the expected end date. When I enrolled at Central Michigan University in 2003, I expected to graduate in 2007 - and I did. Next, I went on to graduate school at Wayne State University in 2007 and I knew I would graduate with my Masters of Social Work degree in 2009 - and I did. Working with an end date in mind is applicable for goals, but I would soon learn the Lord's timeline did not require my authorization or approval.

It was in the year 2008 that waiting became difficult for me, because I had a vision for my life, but no date attached. Instead of seeking the Lord for my next steps, I began to make my own decisions based on what I wanted or felt I needed at that moment. I remember the Lord telling me, "No" regarding my plans for the marriage. Despite the warning signs, I proceeded to go through with it because I equated love and acceptance to marriage and family. I also believed I would be married at a young age and was right on track with my plan, but it wasn't God's plan. I began to follow cultural norms for what my life was supposed to look like. I did not consider that perhaps the Lord had a different plan for me, with a different timeframe.

Ten years later, I found myself, once again, hurrying to move forward in areas of my life prematurely. I was ready for the husband, the home, the family, and the career. There was no doubt the Lord wanted all these things for me and much more. I knew what the Lord had shown me concerning all these areas of my life, so I felt confident that what I wanted was in alignment with what He wanted for me, yet I still had to wait for it.

It Will Be Worth the Wait

I was driving from San Antonio back to Dallas, Texas

on June 21, 2015, when the Lord showed me three distinct visions and revealed to me what they meant. The visions took place in a restaurant setting and here is what I saw:

There was a woman at a salad bar surrounded by strangers; a woman with friends sharing appetizers; and a woman, sitting alone reading a book at an upscale restaurant. The Lord began to reveal to me that at a salad bar the options are limited and the items are often picked over as people take what they want and leave behind what they don't. When going to a salad bar, you opt for convenience over customization. The Lord began to show me that filling up on appetizers has the potential to ruin your appetite for your entrée. Appetizers have a way of making you think you are full, but it is typically short lived because of the lack of nutrients. The woman sat alone at a table with white linen and fine china. She was poised and unbothered as she patiently waited. Her meal was covered by a dome and it was obvious she was satisfied as she ate it all. I imagined it was seasoned to perfection and prepared just the way she had requested it. The Lord began to tell me that He was preparing something special for me and that it would be well worth the wait.

Whatcha' Doing While You Wait?
The Lord promises to give us the desires of our heart

when we delight ourselves in Him (Psalm 37:4), but He does not tell us how long it will take for us to receive those promises. I am a girl with a crazy kind of faith and I literally believe God will do exactly what He has promised. My problem was that I wanted to know all the details and the expected date, which was rarely, if ever, given to me. As I began to delight myself in the Lord, He began to replace the things I thought I wanted with His perfect plans for me. He knew what was best for me even when I could not see it. The Lord is sovereign and all knowing. He will not keep good things from those who walk upright before Him according to Psalm 84:11. This also meant He would not give His children things that would harm them or take them away from Him.

I wish I could tell you that from June 2015 I always waited patiently like the elegant woman in my vision, but that is far from the truth. Many times, I had a really bad attitude regarding the waiting process. I even threw temper tantrums when I didn't get my way and would pout - like that was going to change God's mind. It sounds silly to say, but there were times I even tried to reason with God. I tried to convince Him that my plans were good; to convince Him to fulfill my desires when I wanted them. Sounds silly that I would try to reason with the Lord of Lords and King of Kings, but yep, I have tried it.

We sing songs and make declarations that the Lord

is head of our lives and that our lives are not our own. Yet, here I was making my own plans without even acknowledging my Lord and Savior. I had become consumed with what I wanted and assumed He would simply agree with me. I forgot that I was created by God for His will and His good pleasure (Philippians 2:3). Understanding that the Lord was not trying to hold my blessings hostage, I repented and began to seek Him out and I was concerned with His plan for my life. I was finally ready to surrender the plan I had for my own life.

I began to examine my behavior when I did not get my way, and for the first time I had to acknowledge I was a bit of a brat. People had told me that, but I thought they were being dramatic. Looking at the girl in the mirror was not a pretty picture, but I had to accept the reality that she, was indeed me. I can remember one day in prayer, the Lord showed me the cycle of my behavior when I felt like I was waiting too long for something; especially if there seemed to be no reason for the delay.

When I didn't get my way, I became:

I discovered the root of my behavior was fear and lack of control. With most issues in life, I was able to plan it out to the date of completion, but when it came to the promises of God, there were no end dates given and His word had to be my only proof.

Walking by faith would be much easier if I knew how many miles I had to walk, but it doesn't work like that. I had already seen what happened to my life when I tried to help God, so I decided I had better figure out a way to just be still and wait. I'll be the first to admit, it's easier said than done. And, if I am being completely honest with you girlfriend, my behavior cycle still creeps up and I have to fight back using the word of God.

Still Waiting

After completing my first 5K race on September 3, 2016, the Lord showed me a vision I'll never forget. This is what He showed me:

There was a woman sitting in a restaurant waiting for the order she had requested. As she waited, she began to notice that others were coming in after her, also seated, were receiving their orders before she did. She observed the individuals coming in for takeout, picking up their order and leaving out. All the while, she still waited. She became irritated.

I was a bit puzzled to say the least and I remember asking the Lord what He was trying to tell me with this vision. The Holy Spirit began to reveal to me that some orders require more preparation before they are served. A filet requires more time than a side salad but the wait will be well worth it. I was so excited about this revelation! I thought, somehow, this meant the wait was over.

I started getting my nails done faithfully so I could be ready to say "I do" and rock my new engagement ring, when the man I was seeing at the time popped the big question. We had been building our friendship for over two years and the timing just seemed right. We were talking about wedding dates, areas where we wanted to live even picking names for our future children. I enrolled in a first-time home buyer's program and started saving money so I could be ready. On August 12, 2017 I sat on the floor of a small church in the midst of a worship service when I heard the Lord say, *"I know you're getting impatient, but just know I am not preparing a salad type of blessing for you. I am good for my promises".* During that service, I received a message from my real-estate agent with a home that had just listed and I knew it was going to be my home. On August 13, 2017 I put an offer in on the house and it was accepted. I had always envisioned buying my first home with my husband, so imagine my surprise when I closed on my house, two months later, as an unmarried woman. I didn't quite understand the route the Lord was taking me on and why I still lacked something I deeply desired; marriage.

    I found myself on that emotional behavioral cycle again and one particular time I even tried to offer the Lord my sales pitch on why it would be better for me to be married than single. I promise this really happened. I was sitting in church praying, or if I am being honest, trying to make a proposal to the Lord. I was trying to convince God that it would be better for me to be married, so I did not have to worry about falling into sexual sin. I love that I can talk to the Lord about all things and He will talk back. I had not ever had a conversation with the Lord quite like this one, but it was clear that, regardless what I was talking about, the Lord was not going to move or allow anything to happen until He saw fit. The conversation between the Lord and I went just like this:

Daniellie: Lord, it only makes sense for us to just go ahead and get married. I know he is the one you have for me, so I need for you to release the marriage. It would be better on multiple levels if we were married. We wouldn't have to worry about falling into sexual sin and we can advance the kingdom together through our marriage ministry. We would be able to do more together than single.

The Lord: *It doesn't work like that! Should I just give you the rewards because you simply cannot follow the rules? Because you can't wait for me to approve it, I should move faster to accommodate you and your needs? Sex within a marriage isn't a sin, but should I give you a fast-forward card even though I know you will suffer in the long run? You'll be able to be intimate, but because there are some holes remaining in you, it will cause you to despise one another. Since you just cannot wait a little while longer for a lifetime of companionship, should I grant you temporary pleasures that will leave you both dissatisfied?*

Daniellie: (Shocked at the Lord's response) Who would choose any of these? Not me.

The Lord: *Not with your words, but in your actions you did.* (He softly responded back) *Daughter, wait for me! I've got you covered. Do it simply because I said it. Believe me in this area just like you believe me for what you're expecting me to do. You ask me to do the impossible, but when I ask you to do something you seem to think it's optional.*

I had not considered the implications of my behavior and impatience unto the Lord. He is the creator of all things including me and my life, yet there I was trying to convince Him that my plan was better. The Lord is all-knowing and all-powerful and I know His plans for me exceed my wildest dreams. This conversation with my heavenly Father helped keep me together, but it also left me feeling so thankful that the Lord was kind enough to talk with me in a way I could understand and receive.

Finally, Waiting with Patience

On December 31, 2018, I found myself confident and content, knowing the Lord will deliver every promise He has ever made regardless of how long it takes. I wasn't sure what obstacles were ahead, but I was determined to wait on the Lord. I know the vision is for an appointed time and when it seems like it has been delayed, I will not be anxious because I know that it will surely come, therefore I will wait on it (Habakkuk 2:3).

We have traveled this journey as girlfriends, friends, and now as sisters. I pray you will take responsibility for the heart the Lord has entrusted you with. I hope you will find rest as you wait for the Lord and all the things He has promised you. He is faithful and will fulfill His promise until the return of Christ. An online search of the word, "waiting" is defined as; "The action of staying where one is or delaying action until a particular time or until something else happens". Merriam-Webster defined it like this; "To stay in place in expectation of".

I pray that regardless what you are waiting for, you will continue to trust in His plan and His timing because it is always perfect. I pray the Lord will give you the grace to accept His answer even when it is "No". As we continue to wait with patience, let us remember it's all working for our good and His glory. Know that because He hears you and He loves you, He will work all things together for your good. I pray we will resist the urge to fall into our natural behavioral cycle when we find ourselves waiting longer than we had anticipated. May we rejoice in our continued waiting; knowing that as we wait on the Lord our strength will be renewed and we will mount up with eagle's wings. We will run and not be weary and walk without fainting (Isaiah 40:31). As we wait on the Lord to do exceedingly great things in our lives, I pray you're blown away by what He delivers you. Girlfriend, just wait for it. I know it is going to be so good! It will be better than you could have even imagined and more than you ever asked for.

As I surrendered my fight against the waiting period and became compliant with the process, I began to see that it was all for my protection and His purpose. While I was waiting, He was equipping me for what He had already prepared. The Lord is sovereign and He knows all the details concerning His plan for us and our lives. The Lord knows the exact timing of everything and if we move too swiftly and do our own thing, we forfeit the blessings the Lord had waiting for us. If the Lord has not authorized or approved that thing you desire and are hoping for, just keep waiting. When we possess things prematurely, we run the risk of that thing destroying us. Just like eating a meal that is under-prepared can be poisonous, marrying someone who is unprepared can be dangerous. Trust me, it is better to wait.

Whatever it is you're waiting for, put your trust in God. When it becomes difficult to wait, and it sometimes will, take Him at His word and allow it to be your guiding light. Talk to your Heavenly Father about the issues that flow from your heart because He cares and He is the only one who can actually do anything about the issue anyway. Ask the Lord to give you wisdom and direction concerning the thing you are waiting for. Pursue Him with intentionality and watch and see how He will bring all things to pass in His perfect timing. Waiting on God is our guarantee of victory and I know it will be worth the wait, regardless of how long it takes.

Eyes have not seen it; ears have not heard it and it hasn't even entered into the hearts of men what the Lord has prepared for those who love Him (1 Corinthians 2:9).

A Prayer for My Sisters

Father, I thank you for who you are and the truth of your word. I thank you for being concerned about your children and all the issues that are concerning us. I thank you for being a present help when we're in trouble, even when the trouble is a result of our own decisions. Lord, I pray for my sister that regardless of where she is, or what she has done, she will accept your love and denounce anything that is not like you. You love us, knowing all you know about us, and for that I am thankful. Father I ask that you begin to heal every broken area of my sister's heart. Touch the wounds she may not even know exist. Lord bring clarity and truth where the enemy tried to bring deception and lies. Lord help us stop masking our pain with temporary pleasures. Help us wait on you. Lord help us to trust you even when we cannot trace you. I pray for my sister who is struggling with unforgiveness towards those who hurt her, as well as the unforgiveness she has for herself. Father, I thank you for freedom from our past and for the hope of our future. Help us Lord to give you thanks in ALL things; knowing it is working for our good. Help us to recognize the purpose in our pain and help us to give all glory to your name, no matter the situation. Touch oh Lord, as only you can! Heal, deliver, strengthen, comfort and restore joy and peace like it was never lost. I pray for my sister who may not have a personal relationship with you, and knowingly or unknowingly, put other things and people in a place that is reserved for you. I pray that we will make a conscious choice to become more like you, so that your purpose for our lives may be fulfilled. I believe the best is yet to come, so I thank you in advance! In Jesus name. Amen!

About the Author

Author

Daniellie Marie is a triple threat to the kingdom of darkness as she has yielded herself to the Holy Spirit to be used as a Willing Vessel through singing, writing and speaking. Daniellie knew she was different as a child and desired to be used greatly by God at a young age. But she had no idea of the magnitude in which the Lord would use her life for His glory. She is energized by seeing lives transformed through the word of God.

Daniellie is passionate about education and earned her Bachelor of Science Degree in Psychology from Central Michigan University, and Master of Social Work Degree from Wayne State University. She is a Certified Prevention Specialist with the Michigan Certification Board for Addiction Professionals. She is a Clinical Social Worker serving as a Rehabilitation Specialist and the founder of We Talk, LLC. Daniellie has served as a worship leader in her local church and enjoys volunteering with local youth programs.

Daniellie has a magical way of connecting with people from all walks of life and believes there are no strangers, only friends we haven't met yet. Daniellie is the youngest of three girls, but her sisters call her "grandma", because she has an old soul. Daniellie loves life and the beauty each day has to offer. Her happy place is anywhere with water, a book, good food, music and laughter. In Daniellie's debut book, *"My Heart; My Responsibility: A Single Woman's Guide to Waiting"*, she opens her heart and shares her story of victory despite tragedy. Growing up without her parents; married and divorced before the age of 30, this girl is truly an overcomer. She gives all glory to God for using her transparent story of hope to be an inspiration and guide to other women.

Daniellie waits with great expectation of her future as her life's story continues to unfold; believing the best is yet to come according to Jeremiah 29:11.

Connect with Daniellie Marie:
Email: wetalk@danielliemarie.com
Website: www.danielliemarie.com
Instagram: @daniellie_marie
Facebook: wetalk.danielliemarie

www.ingramcontent.com/pod-product-compliance
Lightning Source LLC
Chambersburg PA
CBHW052103110526
44591CB00013B/2324